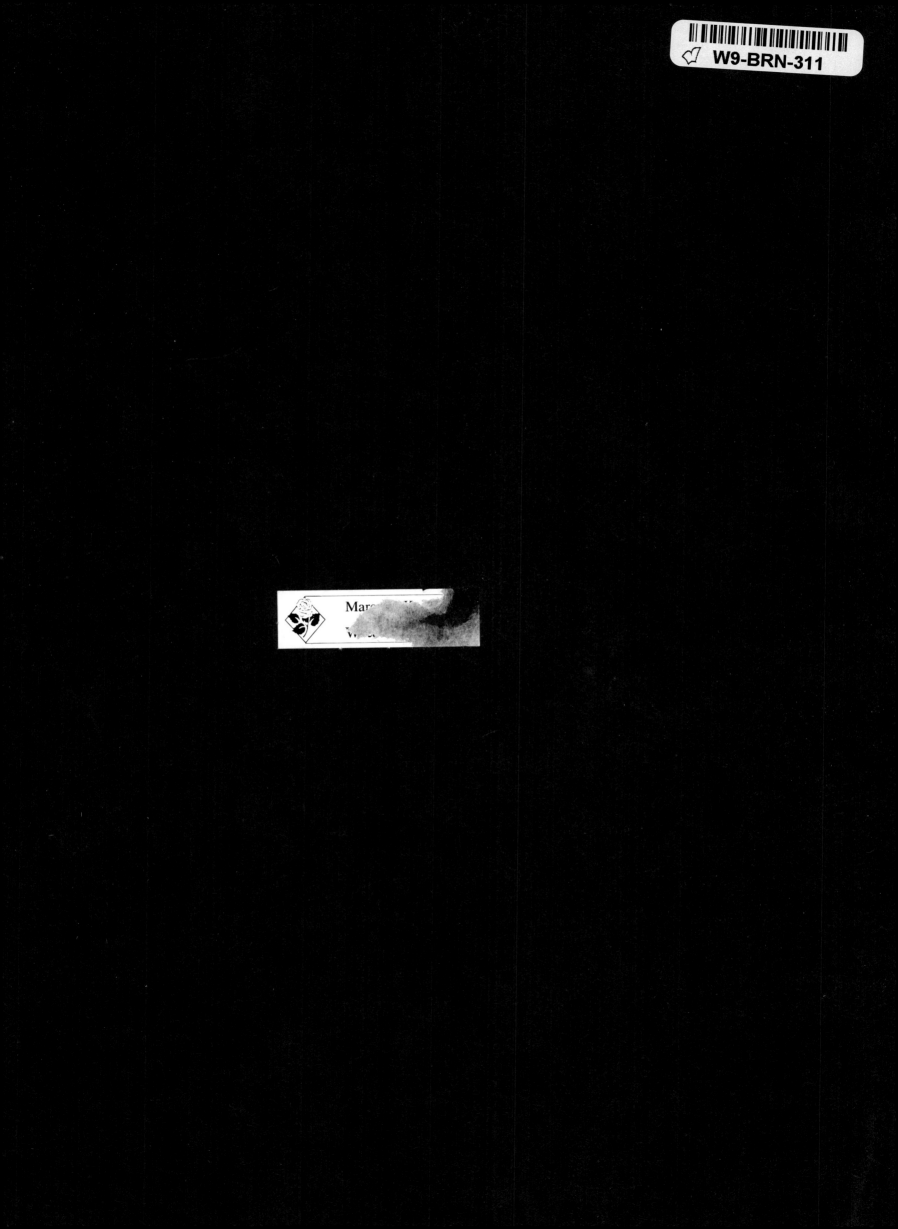

ILLINOIS

ILLINOIS

PHOTOGRAPHY BY GARY IRVING
TEXT BY KRISTINA VALAITIS

GRAPHIC ARTS CENTER PUBLISHING COMPANY
PORTLAND, OREGON

International Standard Book Number 0-932575-68-4
Library of Congress Catalog Number 88-80537
Copyright ©MCMLXXXVIII by Graphic Arts Center Publishing Company
P.O. Box 10306 • Portland, Oregon 97210 • 503/226-2402
Editor-in-Chief • Douglas A. Pfeiffer
Designer • Robert Reynolds
Cartography • Tom Patterson and Manoa Mapworks
Typographer • Harrison Typesetting, Inc.
Printer • Graphic Arts Center, Inc.
Bindery • Lincoln & Allen
Printed in the United States of America

Dedicated to the memory of Christine Sandin

Gary Irving

We wish to thank the following publishers and authors for permission to reprint copyrighted poetry selections and quotations used in the text. The page numbers in parentheses relate to this book.

Excerpts from "Passers-By" (p. 149), "Skyscraper" (p. 141), "Uplands in May" (p. 105), and "I Am the People, the Mob" (p. 41) from CHICAGO POEMS by Carl Sandburg, copyright 1916 by Holt, Rinehart and Winston, Inc., renewed 1944 by Carl Sandburg, reprinted by permission of Harcourt Brace Jovanovich, Inc. Excerpts from "Prairie" (pp. 61, 73, 77), "Loam" (p. 53), and "The Year" (p. 37) from CORNHUSKERS by Carl Sandburg, copyright 1918 by Holt, Rinehart and Winston, Inc., renewed 1946 by Carl Sandburg, reprinted by permission of Harcourt Brace Jovanovich, Inc. Excerpt from "Haze" (p. 57) in SMOKE AND STEEL by Carl Sandburg, copyright 1920 by Harcourt Brace Jovanovich, Inc., renewed 1948 by Carl Sandburg, reprinted by permission of the publisher. Excerpts from "The Windy City" (pp. 133, 153) and "Improved Farm Land" (p. 29) in SLABS OF THE SUNBURNT WEST by Carl Sandburg, copyright 1922 by Harcourt Brace Jovanovich, Inc., renewed 1950 by Carl Sandburg, reprinted by permission of the publisher. Excerpts from "Auburn" (p. 157), "Cornfield Ridge and Stream" (p. 93), and "Timber Moon" (p. 25) from GOOD MORNING, AMERICA by Carl Sandburg, copyright 1928, 1956 by Carl Sandburg, reprinted by permission of Harcourt Brace Jovanovich, Inc. Excerpts from THE PEOPLE, YES (p. 109) by Carl Sandburg, copyright 1936 by Harcourt Brace Jovanovich, Inc., renewed 1964 by Carl Sandburg, reprinted by permission of the publisher. Excerpts from "Alone and Not Alone" (p. 137) and "If So Hap May Be" (p. 121) from HONEY AND SALT, copyright 1963 by Carl Sandburg, reprinted by permission of Harcourt Brace Jovanovich, Inc. Excerpt from "Aerial Photograph" (p. 101) by Bruce Guernsey in BENCHMARK, ANTHOLOGY OF ILLINOIS POETRY, Stormline Press, 1988. Excerpt from "representations of the self" (p. 69) by John Knoepfle in POEMS FROM THE SANGAMON, University of Illinois Press, 1985. Excerpt from WHERE THE SKY BEGAN. LAND OF THE TALLGRASS PRAIRIE (p. 21) by John Madson, Sierra Club Books, 1985. With permission of the Stevenson family, excerpt from Governor Adlai Stevenson's Welcome to the Democratic National Convention (p. 125), 1952.

ILLINOIS

National Wildlife Refuges

Selected State Parks

Controlled Access Highways

Other Major Highways

0 10 20 30 40 50 mi
0 10 20 30 40 50   100 km

Galena
APPLE RIVER CANYON
CHAIN O'LAKES
Fox Lake
ILLINOIS BEACH
Freeport
Rockford
Belvidere
Woodstock
Waukegan
UPPER MISSISSIPPI
MISSISSIPPI PALISADES
WHITE PINES FOREST
DeKalb
Elgin
Highland Park
LAKE MICHIGAN
UPPER MISSISSIPPI
Sterling
Rock River
SHABBONA
Aurora
Wheaton
CHICAGO
Chicago River
SILVER SPRINGS
Mendota
DesPlaines R.
Moline
Peru
STARVED ROCK
Ottawa
Morris
Joliet
Illinois
La Salle
MATTHIESSEN
GOOSE LAKE PRAIRIE
Kewanee
Kankakee
MISSISSIPPI River
MARK TWAIN
Vermilion
Kankakee River
Galesburg
River
Goose Lake
Pontiac
Iroquois R.
IOWA
Monmouth
Peoria
INDIANA
NAUVOO
Pekin
Bloomington
MORAINE VIEW
Rantoul
Macomb
Mackinaw River
CHAUTAUQUA
KICKAPOO
WEINBERG-KING
Crane Lake
Lincoln
WELDON SPRINGS
Champaign
Urbana
MARK TWAIN
La Moine River
Danville
Quincy
Beardstown
LINCOLN'S NEW SALEM
Decatur
WALNUT POINT
SILOAM SPRINGS
MEREDOSIA
Sangamon River
Lake Decatur
Kaskaskia River
MISSOURI
Springfield
Jacksonville
Lake Springfield
Mattoon
MARK TWAIN
Sangchris Lake
Lake Shelbyville
FOX RIDGE
Carlinville
Pana
Illinois
Lake Lou Yaeger
BEAVER DAM
Jerseyville
Coffeen Lake
Effingham
Robinson
MARK TWAIN
Embarras River
PERE MARQUETTE
Vandalia
Alton
Carlyle Lake
STEPHEN A. FORBES
RED HILLS
Missouri River
East St. Louis
ELDON HAZLET
Lawrenceville
Mt. Carmel
Belleville
Little Wabash River
BEALL WOODS
Mt. Vernon
Skillet Fork
Wabash River
Kaskaskia River
Rend Lake
N. Saline River
Ohio River
DuQuoin
Little Muddy River
Benton
Eldorado
Kinkaid Lake
Crab Orchard Lake
Carbondale
Marion
CRAB ORCHARD
GIANT CITY
GARDEN OF THE GODS
CAVE-IN-ROCK
FERNE CLYFFE
Anna
SHAWNEE NATIONAL FOREST
KENTUCKY
Ohio River
MISSOURI
Cairo

N
W E

7

■ *Left:* Once the seat of the Northwest Territory's government, the Cahokia Courthouse (c. 1790) in St. Clair County, is the oldest standing building in the Midwest. ■ *Above:* Route 34 leads to Monmouth, where Wyatt Earp, the famous Wild West marshall, was born. He later heeded the advice: "Go West, Young Man, Go West."

■ *Above:* The annual Hot-Air Balloon Rally near Danville in Vermilion County continues a century-old sight-seeing tradition.
■ *Right:* Illinois continues to be a vital commercial transportation center. The Railway Museum in Union in Kane County displays trolleys and other emblems of the state's railway heritage.

■ *Left:* The Sauk and Fox Indians held lands along the Rock River until they were forced farther west by settlers in 1832. ■ *Above:* Jutting five-eighths of a mile into Lake Michigan, Navy Pier has a maritime history as a dock for ocean-going vessels; recently, however, it has become a stunning setting for cultural events.

■ *Left:* A grain elevator rises like a proud monument above the neatly plowed fields in Moultrie County, standing sentinel over the agricultural landscape. ■ *Above:* Because much of southern Illinois is south of the Mason-Dixon line, fall's primary colors—sky blue, maple red and yellow—arrive late, and spring blooms early.

■ Prairie dropseed, *sporobolus heterolepis*, can be found in restored prairies such as the Schulenberg Prairie at the Morton Arboretum near Lisle in DuPage County. This thirty-acre restoration is a living natural community with two hundred species of prairie plants and is one of the arboretum's most heavily visited sites.

THE CONTOURS OF PLACE

Illinois. Ask Illinoisans what their state means to them, and you will hear first about the parts they know best—a stretch of blacktop that promises "home soon" in Jo Daviess County, the marriage of two powerful rivers downstate in "Egypt," or the sun poised on the gentlest rise of a field in Champaign County at day's end. You might hear about jogging along Chicago's incomparable lakefront—its "Riviera"—or about watching the fireworks along with five hundred thousand "neighbors" in Grant Park on the Fourth of July. Stories like these, fragments of place, begin to evoke Illinois today.

But Illinois as the Prairie State? There is no one left to tell firsthand of crossing the inland prairie by celestial navigation or by the compass plants, which were used by pioneers to mark the edges of wagon routes. No historical photos survive to suggest the power of the tall grass billowing like the sea for fifty miles in all directions. With the right questions, however, this memory and many others can be coaxed from the land that holds them.

To make sense of Illinois today is to tell a story that includes a small town called Metropolis at the southern tip of the state—and the actual metropolis of Chicago, in whose shadow a suburban galaxy continues to expand. In pioneer Illinois the story was reversed. Shawneetown—a thriving gateway to the frontier on the Ohio River—overshadowed Chicago, which was little more than a trading post until 1850. Yet the population of this outpost—situated where a sluggish river entered Lake Michigan—doubled and tripled like yeast dough during the last half of the nineteenth century.

In the eighteenth century, stories of Illinois would have been told in Spanish, French, and English, for in succession these colonial powers claimed and lost Illinois for their regents. At that time, the native tongues belonged to the Indian nations that competed with white settlers in Illinois and lost, migrating even farther west. These Indian nations were the Sauk, the Fox, and the Illiniwek—which included the Potawatomi, Peoria, Kaskaskia, Cahokia, and Tamaroa tribes. It was for the Illiniwek that the French named the state.

Indian cultures had also flourished from 2000 B.C. to approximately A.D. 1500—long before Jolliet, Père Marquette, and La Salle plied Illinois rivers by canoe and explored its ancient hunting trails and trade paths. The Woodland, Hopewell, and Mississippian cultures, which had existed in pre-Columbian Illinois, disappeared just as Europeans set foot on the Eastern Seaboard.

The topography of Illinois retains traces of the interaction of those successive societies with the land. Some of the earliest cultures left such impressive marks on the landscape as the earth mounds at Cahokia. But these cultures were no match for the nineteenth-century settlers who, in the process of creating the state, became a force for change almost equal to the natural forces of geology that had shaped the land slowly over millions of years.

As we stand with our feet planted firmly on the ground of an electronic age, the creeping, yet inexorable, pace of the glaciers—not to mention the duration of their impact—is hard to fathom. Yet from the vantage point of a weather satellite 438 miles above the earth in near-polar orbit, the role of continental glaciers in creating Illinois and the whole Midwest begins to seem plausible. From there, the man-made geometry of skylines, county roads, and fence-posts gives way to the irregularity and sinuousness of natural features shaped by water, wind, and crushing, mile-high glaciers. The result: Moraines and palisades are in bas relief, the brows of hills and dunes set back from graceful arcs of lakeshore.

As a physical land mass, Illinois can be located largely by natural borders. The Mississippi River forms all 570 miles of its western border. Its southern tip is the confluence of two major rivers, the Ohio and the Mississippi. Its northeastern border is a sixty-three mile crescent of Lake Michigan's shore. This cradle of river and lake shore is a good point of departure for a careful consideration of the state's natural landscape.

Illinois, population 11,426,518, stretches 380 miles—from 37 to 42 degrees north latitude. Pine trees grow at its northern border, and cotton fields at its southern. The Chicago metropolitan area is slightly farther north than New York City, and downstate Cairo is farther south than Richmond, Virginia—that is, 150 miles *south of* the Mason-Dixon line. At 1,241 feet above sea level, Charles Mound in Jo Daviess County, is the state's highest point. Cairo is the lowest, at 268 feet. In the Shawnee Hills in the south, 800 feet separate the highest point from the lowest. Still, the reports are true, the state is generally flat.

During the Ice Age, most of Illinois was covered at some point by one or another of the continental glaciers. These mile-high sheets of ice created the topography of Illinois. Scenic ridges, called moraines, were formed when the glaciers paused in their retreat. The high-relief hills of the northwestern, southwestern, and southern parts of the state remained intact—miraculously untouched by the ancient glacial drifts which flattened the state's vast interior. Depressions were filled with a loose carpet of post-glacial till above the bedrock, and then covered with loess—the yellowish-brown dust left from glacial deposits and carried across the land by the wind. These deposits gave Illinois the soil rich in soluble minerals and plant foods that promised its future as an agricultural state.

One glacier that descended and retreated from fifty thousand to one hundred twenty-five thousand years ago was so pervasive in the state that geologists named it the Illinoisan. Advancing over areas scraped previously by the Nebraskan and Kansan glaciers, the Illinoisan reached almost to what is now the Ohio River, leaving the three most hilly areas of the state untouched. The Wisconsin Drift was the last glacier to sculpt Illinois, by most accounts retreating a mere fifteen thousand years ago—a geological blink of an eye. Its southernmost reach is marked by the Shelbyville moraine, which divides the state north and south and allows for speculation about geology as destiny. Above the moraine, the soil is deep, level, and well-watered; below it, the land is rugged with hills. The state's original development as an industrial region began north of the

moraine; south of it, the state remained rural. The Mason-Dixon line runs remarkably close to this natural divide. As the weather changed and the Wisconsin drift melted, it created what is now Lake Michigan, along with the largest river system in Illinois.

The rivers that border Illinois, in addition to the one that traverses it for 300 miles linking the Great Lakes to the Gulf of Mexico, made Illinois an inevitable crossroads for everyone traveling north, south, east, or west in the new land. These arteries of trade and transportation put Illinois at the heart of a larger drama—the young nation's economic, geographic, and cultural expansion. Thus, Illinois became a cauldron of values, as well. To evoke Illinois in geographical terms alone, therefore, is to miss the mythical power of the state. Men and women created Illinois as a state with social, political, and economic dimensions as well. The political borders of Illinois were not set until that statehood occurred in 1818. Politics being politics encourages speculation about the inclusion of a certain community that became the third largest city in the country. What would have happened if Illinois had come into the Union as it had been as a territory, that is, without a certain trading post founded by Jean Baptiste Point du Sable? Yet the Illinois that came into the Union on December 3, 1818, as the twenty-first state, with a population variously reported as 20,000, 35,000, and 60,000, did contain that community that is home to more than three million people today. The fact that this metropolis is Chicago, Illinois—and not Chicago, Wisconsin—is due to the efforts of Nathaniel Pope, an Illinois territorial legislator, and his nephew, Daniel Pope Cook. They persuaded Congress to adopt an amendment to the U.S. Congressional Enabling Act of August 16, 1818, which redrew the northern border of territorial Illinois.

The early settlers of Illinois began to see themselves as the sons and daughters of a place that—although not quite the Eden its promoters had touted—was still large enough for the love of liberty to grow. Illinois was a place where cultures clashed; yet it was large

■ *Union County has a full-blown southern spring weeks before buds flower at the state's northern border. In the Trail of Tears State Park, dogwood blooms as early and luxuriantly as in Dixie.*

enough for ideas to be tested and then discarded or transplanted, a place where religious experiments could fail or flourish. This sense of place was buttressed by geography and geology.

Below the glacial drift is, of course, bedrock that contains bituminous coal, natural gas, crude oil, clay and stone, as well as fluorspar, which is the state mineral. Deposited more than two hundred million years ago across two-thirds of Illinois, the state's bituminous coal makes up 10 percent of the nation's total coal deposits. Quarries of limestone and dolomite are found in what was once the floor of an ancient ocean that covered most of Illinois millions of years ago. The sand, gravel, and crushed stone found throughout the state were laid down by the meltwaters of the glaciers and are now sold for use in construction. Nationwide, Illinois ranks first in the production of silica sand, found primarily in La Salle and Ogle counties and used in the manufacture of glass and for grinding and polishing.

Although pre-Columbian effigy pendants made of the state mineral, fluorspar, have been found in Illinois, this mineral is now thought to be too brittle for jewelry. This is unfortunate, when one sees its crystalline range of colors—from white to purple, to pink, yellow, green and tan. Originally mined in the mid-nineteenth century for the galena—a lead ore found with it—fluorspar is now sought for use in the production of aluminum, rocket fuels, and in fluorides—which in turn are used in toothpaste, non-stick coatings, and in plastics. Illinois accounts for more than 50 percent of the nation's total production of this valuable mineral.

Without the presence of clay, even less would be known about the earliest cultures in Illinois than is known today. Indians of the Woodland and Mississippian periods left both ceremonial and utilitarian pottery behind. The presence of clay, deposited near the surface of the land during the glacial movements, also attracted immigrants, especially nineteenth-century potters from England. Potteries were a significant industry in Illinois in the 1840s, filling early settlers' needs for jugs, crocks, pitchers, bricks, and drainage tiles. There were brickyards in Alton, Quincy, and Jacksonville, as well as Chicago. Rumor has it that Illinois bricks, put on barges and floated down the Mississippi River to the Gulf of Mexico, helped to build the Panama Canal.

Illinoisans today, conditioned by the great stories of the wilderness west of the Rocky Mountains, find it difficult to comprehend the way in which nineteenth-century Illinois inspired the romantic imagination. "The wilds of Illinois," which contained the "grandest objects of nature," symbolized nature untouched and untrammeled by mankind in *Lodore*, a novel by Mary Shelley, wife of the poet, Percy Shelley. But this vision of Illinois was not just a figment of Shelley's imagination, as was Frankenstein's monster which was perhaps her most memorable character. There was a wildness and lushness there, according to the accounts of many early settlers.

When the early settlers encountered the vast interior grassland of Illinois with its expansive sky above, they stepped into a dramatic natural epic already in progress: "the silent struggle between trees and grass," as John Madson put it in *Where the Sky Began*," lasting twenty-five million years in one form or another across a broad battlefront." Put simply, Illinois was a crossroads between woodlands and the treeless plains of the West. The alternating rhythm of cool and warm weather after the last glacial retreat encouraged forests when the climate was moist and cool and discouraged them when the climate was drier and warmer. The pervasive tall grass, especially resistant to heat and drought, was thus also resistant to fires ignited by accident or design, by bolts of lightning or Indians.

In 1791, long before Illinois reached statehood, Captain Thomas Morris was a spectator for this drama, noting that the summer prairie presented "one of the most delightful prospects I have ever beheld; all the low grounds being meadow, and without wood, and all of the high grounds being covered with trees and appearing like islands; the whole scene seemed an elysium."

■ *More than 40 percent of Illinois was forested with maple, oak, hickory, beech, and tulip poplar before settlement, but only 25 percent of that remains as old growth timber today.*

In some ways, this competition between forest and prairie was critical to the early settlers who did not ask, "Why prairie?" but rather wondered, "Why not trees?" The wrong question delayed settlement for years. Because pioneers skirted the tall grass to live on and cultivate land near woodlands and along rivers, the great central portion of the state, though arguably the most fertile, was the last to come under the plow. In 1849, for example, fourteen million acres, nearly 40 percent of the land area in Illinois, was still in the possession of the federal government. Most of it was prairie. Illinois was thus filled from the bottom up, like a rain barrel whose sides were the banks of the three boundary rivers. The American bottom, an alluvial plain of great fertility that ran along the Mississippi from Alton to Chester for one hundred miles, as well as bottomland along the Illinois and Wabash rivers, gave easterners the first clue to the value of Illinois soil. In time the belief that the prairie could not be farmed, unless next to woodland, lost its hold as mysteriously as it had taken root.

Illinois still contains a great variety of natural areas: forests, prairies, savannas, wetlands, lakes and ponds, streams, caves, rocky glades, and beaches. However, the forces of settlement have been so pervasive that few of the natural areas present at the time of settlement have survived in their original condition. Before Illinois was settled, forests covered 40 percent of the land, or about 13.8 million acres. Forests today account for only 10 percent of the landscape. Forested land that has not fallen to the logger or farmer includes oak, hickory, white pine, bald cypress, and tupelo gum. However, the greatest loss has been even the memory of the prairie. Tallgrass prairie once covered nearly 55 percent of the state, roughly twenty million acres. Today, not even 1 percent of Illinois land remains prairie, usually in relicts in cemeteries, along old railroad rights of way, or in prairie restoration projects or preserves.

As these natural settings have changed, so have the flora and fauna in Illinois. The bison, mountain lion, and bear are long gone, but Illinois still has white-tailed deer, rabbit, and pheasant. Its ponds, lakes, streams, and rivers are still host to hundreds of fish and wildlife species. Approximately four hundred thousand hunters and one and one-half million anglers enjoy their sports in Illinois annually. The state is a crossroads for waterfowl migrating through the Midwest. Adult bald eagles, the national symbol, winter in Illinois along the Mississippi River. Each year one hundred thousand Canada geese migrate to Horseshoe Lake Wildlife Refuge. Colonies of great blue heron can be seen nesting there in the Heron Pond Nature Preserve. The diverse natural heritage of the state today can be experienced in more than one hundred state parks and conservation areas, many in southern Illinois, such as Shawnee National Forest in the Illinois "Ozarks," Ferne Clyffe State Park, Beall Woods—noted for some of the oldest trees in Illinois—and in Giant City State Park.

Did Captain Morris behold a sea of grass with islands of trees, or an advancing forest enclosing inlets and small bays of grass? In some ways, it did not matter. The ancient competition between forest and prairie was the backdrop for new struggles in Illinois, a state which was, in turn, a romantic wilderness, a new frontier, and finally, the Prairie State, with some of the most fertile soil in the world under that sea of grass, waiting to be discovered.

The natural landscape of Illinois is surprisingly varied—with the Shawnee Hills, the Mississippi River bluffs, the Lake Michigan shoreline with beaches and dunes, scenic rivers, streams, wetlands, and even a cypress swamp. Yet it is the undeniably flat central region that has dubbed Illinois "The Prairie State." To look at the miles of cultivated land in central Illinois today and say "prairie" is to come to the theatre as the final curtain drops and say "great performance." The prairie encountered by Père Marquette, La Salle, Morris Birkbeck, and Eliza Farnham now survives only in their journals, diaries, and in rare relics. Yet, like a bloom in a bulb, the idea of the prairie infused the culture of Illinois with an open spirit that may fade or flourish, but ever persists.

■ *Rapelling enthusiasts sometimes enjoy their sport on the rugged cliffs in Ferne Clyffe State Park. Nearby Shawnee National Forest attracts hikers, botanists, birdwatchers, and campers.*

There is a way the moon understands the hoot owl
Sitting on an arm of a sugar maple throwing its
One long lonesome cry up the ladders of the moon—
There is a way the moon finds company early in the fall-time.

CARL SANDBURG

Moonrise, suburban DuPage County

■ *Left:* At Starved Rock State Park near Ottawa, eighteen miles of trails link waterfalls, canyons, caves, bluffs, and narrow gorges in nine hundred acres of wildlands. ■ *Above:* Rock River flows near the Quad-Cities: Iowa's Davenport and the Illinois cities of Moline, East Moline, and Rock Island, once the most active river port in Illinois.

Here the roots of a half mile of trees
    dug their runners deep in the loam
    for a grip and a hold against wind storms.
Then the axmen came and the chips flew
    to the zing of steel and handle—
    the lank railsplitters cut the big ones first,
    the beeches and the oaks, then the brush.

CARL SANDBURG

Rural woodland, Clay County

■ *Above:* Untouched by the continental glaciers that covered most of Illinois millions of years ago, the Garden of the Gods is noted for its rock formations. ■ *Right:* Created from the Big Muddy and Casey Fork rivers, Rend Lake—with its 162 miles of shoreline—provides crappie, bass, and catfish for anglers in southern Illinois.

■ *Left:* Once, such flowers as marsh phlox dotted the summer tall-grass prairie; today, only about two thousand acres remain to give meaning to the state's nickname, "The Prairie State." ■ *Above:* Over one hundred thousand Canada geese migrate to the wildlife refuge at Horseshoe Lake Conservation Area every year.

■ *Left:* Eight hundred feet separate the highest and lowest points in the Illinois Ozarks. ■ *Above:* Prairie dock and prairie dropseed are native to the prairie that once covered more than half the state. By late autumn, successive kinds of prairie flowers have bloomed and faded; and grasses have been bleached by the sun.

A storm of white petals,
Buds throwing open baby fists
Into hands of broad flowers.

CARL SANDBURG

Shawnee National Forest

■ *Left:* Named for its salt deposits, Saline County is also one of the major coal-producing counties in the state. ■ *Above:* A county of contrasts, DuPage is one of the fastest developing areas in the state. It still surprises with its open fields contrasting sharply with nearby shopping malls and corporate headquarters.

I am the seed ground.
    I am a prairie that will stand for much plowing.
    Terrible storms pass over me.
    I forget.

CARL SANDBURG

Approaching storm, Union County

Illinois still contains the vast panoramas that are captured in the early accounts of its landscape. But now the thousands of acres exposed to the eye are of corn and soybeans, not meadows of grass and flowers. With more than half its population occupying little more than a tenth of its geographical area, the landscape of Illinois remains predominantly rural and surprisingly varied—with rolling hills, river palisades, and forests, as well the state's flattest land in Douglas County, where a marble needs more than a gentle push to roll anywhere. Surprising as the range of the state's contours may be, the landscape in central Illinois—with its horizontal vistas foiled by clusters of farm buildings, houses square to the road, and grain elevators that rise like great monuments in the distance—remains emblematic of rural Illinois.

Once upon a time, it was this land that was the "far west" for a new and expansive nation. If the camera had been part of the pioneers' gear, there is no doubt it would have been used to take the measure of what would become a mythic prairie and capture its unexpected scale. Even heroes larger than life would have had to mount a horse to see over the prairie grass. Perhaps even the famous Marshall Earp, born in Monmouth, Illinois, would have posed for a snapshot in his home state, knotting the eight-foot-tall prairie grass over the pommel of his saddle, his feet in stirrups that brushed a carpet of prairie flowers and grasses as he rode into the sunset to seek his fortune even farther west. Would stories of pioneer Illinois rank with the rough-and-ready tales of the cowboy west if historic photos survived of the endless prairies, as they swept away from the camera's eye toward the quiet level where sky and land meet?

Would more of the Illinois prairie have been preserved if it had been captured as the romantic wilderness it was by the wet-plate photographic process, which helped to make the Wild West into a symbol? Certainly photographers played a historic role in documenting the final act in the country's western expansion. More than that, however, their photos—of areas such as Yellowstone and the Rocky Mountains, for example—made these wonders "real" for the public who, through Congress, later preserved them as national parks. By all accounts, the prairies were a surprising landscape. But the early settlers' and travelers' views of this startlingly open land were carried back east and abroad by descriptions alone. Their journals and letters have to contain the prairie for us today as well.

The word "prairie" is French for meadow and suggests the absence of trees, a notion reflected in a dispatch from Louis Jolliet dated August 1, 1674: "At first, when we were told of these treeless lands, I imagined that it was a country ravaged by fire, where the soil was so poor that it could produce nothing. But we have certainly observed the contrary; and no better soil can be found either for corn, for vines, or for any fruit whatever." Like other explorers, Jolliet carried a mental landscape with him, and consequently, could not imagine a treeless plain as the natural state of the land he eventually deemed incomparable for growing vines or fruit or grain. Little could Jolliet guess at this point that prairies were not "ravaged" by fire, but rather maintained—some say created—by fire. When the earliest pioneer impressions were recorded, there were no analogues in Europe or along the Eastern Seaboard for the vast stretches of grassland the settlers would find as they moved westward from the forest shadows to the sunlit prairie. Early chroniclers of this landscape resorted to metaphors of "garden," "meadow," "flowered carpet"—exploring their future with images in which they had fixed their past. And they needed "ocean" to convey the surprising scale of their view. As Eliza Farnham wrote in 1846, in her *Life in Prairie Land*:

> To travel . . . for days and even weeks, your steed never tiring, your speed never flagging, is to gather an idea of vastness unparalleled except upon the ocean. Firm, inhabitable vastness, every foot of which is teeming with the energies that support life; every acre of which would yield an ample subsistence to large numbers of the famishing and perishing thousands of the crowded old world.

■ *Sunflowers grow well in Grundy County. The Grundy County Corn Festival is one of the many summer celebrations of the state's agricultural prowess—culminating in the state fair.*

Early writers referred to the trees that sometimes intruded in the grassland as "islands in the ocean." The woodland at the edge of the prairie was the "shore of a lake indented with deep vistas, like bays and inlets, and throwing out long points, like capes and headlands," according to one early gazetteer. But it was for the waves of grass that bent sinuously in the wind that the prairie was compared to a "sea of grass." Adrift with no view of shore, the pioneers were as reliant upon star charts as they crossed the prairie as was Columbus in search of the New World by sea.

Understandably, the prairie in summer required the most flowery language. For some, prairies equalled the finest English parks or they matched fabled gardens, possessing a "beauty we can scarce imagine to have been surpassed by Eden itself," as Eliza Farnham exclaimed. The prairie in summer was also exotic, an Oriental rug of grass and flowers, spilling out before the traveler "in which a ground of lively green is ornamented with a profusion of the gaudiest hues, and fringed with a rich border of forest and thicket," as James Hall, an early writer, suggested in his short story, "The Indian Hater."

The mood of the prairie changed dramatically with the seasons, both in scale and color. Through spring and summer, smaller flowers gave way to taller and larger ones; grasses also grew taller and changed color, green hues giving way to yellows, russets, and wines in the autumn. The prairie's poetry is contained in the flowers, the names themselves metaphors that stir the imagination. In spring came the earliest prairie flowers—pasqueflower or "windflowers," white or lavender on slender stems, the prairie anemones; then "prairie smoke," white to lavender, tulip-like; buttercup; and wild violet. Next came Indian paintbrush; marsh marigold; and yellow star grass, almost a daffodil; wild strawberry; and blue-eyed grass, a shy iris. Then came the taller summer flowers—daisies; larkspur; purple coneflower; and wild roses. By July, the prairie was vivid with red-orange Turk's cap lilies, forty blooms on an eight-foot-tall stem; wild orchids; goldenrod; ironweed; asters; sunflowers; and compass plants, whose stalks pioneers used to mark the edges of wagon routes. In August, the prairie filled with blazing star, with its rose-purple blossoms that burst low or high on a six-foot spike. By the first frost, the prairie flowers faded while the grasses turned to wine, russet, and bronze before winter's descent.

There was a disquieting beauty on the prairie, as well. By late autumn, the grasses and flowers had dried into tinder that could be ignited into wildfire. James Hall's short story, "The Dark Maid of Illinois," captures the awe and fear wrought by another mood of the sea of grass in which "the whole line of horizon was clothed with flames that rolled around, and curled, and dashed upward like the angry waves of a burning ocean . . . having the appearance of angry billows of a fiery liquid, dashing against each other, and foaming, and throwing flakes of burning spray into the air."

Far from killing the prairie, such fires maintained and perpetuated it. The natural landscape of Illinois would have been forests without the "red buffalo," as the Indians referred to these rampant prairie fires common as bison on the prairie. Safe from the flames that moved as fast as the wind in autumn and early spring, the prairie's life—its roots and reproductive system—was protected under the sod. Trees could not survive the heat of the fire, but prairie grasses and forbs rose spectacularly and vigorously from the ashes. With the dried grasses gone, the sun penetrated the sod more directly, and the rain moistened it more thoroughly.

Hardy big bluestem, the dominant grass in any authentic prairie, can outreach a man's grasp easily, even as its roots sometimes plunge fifteen feet below the surface. Years of growth and regrowth produced a mineral-rich sod of fabled fertility. One-half square meter of big bluestem sod, for example, may contain miles of the most intricate root system. Once discovered, word went out that the Grand Prairie was the land of Canaan. Its treelessness became a highly touted advantage, as promoters began their campaigns: "In no part of the U.S. can uncultivated land be made into farms with

less labor than Illinois." Thus, as the prairie gave purpose to the plow, it was the plow that hastened the disappearance of the prairie.

As the days of one of the nation's most historic landscapes became numbered, the foundation for the state's agricultural economy was laid. Natural conditions favor farming in Illinois. The land is level or rolling, the soil among the most productive in the world—the legacy of the prairie and the glacier. During the summer, fulfillment of the promise of that land can be seen on any road throughout the central part of the state. At that time of year, Illinois is all corn and soybeans. Together, these crops account for 87 percent of the crop sales in Illinois. Four-fifths of the geographic area of Illinois is farmland on which corn, soybeans, and wheat are primarily harvested. Each year, Illinois is either first or second in production of corn, soybean, and hogs; and it leads the nation in the value of crops marketed.

Even Illinoisans can be surprised by the variety of crops grown throughout the state—watermelons, popcorn, sweet peppers, cantaloupes, and pecans. Horseradish, a pungent root which brings tears of joy to the eyes as it adds zest to sauces and sausages, is an important crop in St. Clair and Madison counties, where more than two-thirds of the nation's horseradish is grown. Still harvested largely by hand, horseradish plants today are derived from original root cuttings brought to Illinois by nineteenth-century European immigrants. Farther south in "Egypt," orchards of pear, plum, cherry, apple and peach trees bloom fragrantly in the spring. In Union and Jackson counties, one-quarter of all Illinois apples—delicious, golden delicious, and Jonathan primarily— and almost one-half of all the state's peaches are grown. While fruits and vegetables allow Illinois farmers to diversify, they are planted only on one percent of the crop land in the state, no competition for corn which is planted on more than twelve million acres.

These acres of corn could not have grown so well without the forbs and grasses, such as big bluestem, of the precedent prairie gardens. The open vista of countless rows of eight-foot-tall corn stalks can still evoke some sense of the tall grass which once carpeted the prairie. However, the *trompe l'oeil* conceals an important distinction. The prairie was a complex natural community that replicated itself each year, its plants perennial with intricate root systems that fostered a mineral-rich soil. The cultivated agricultural landscape is distinguished by crops of corn and soybeans, annuals which draw nutrients from a soil that needs to be renewed to stem erosion. Still, this cultivated landscape in its turn elicits a range of responses in contemporary observers, as did the prairie more than one hundred fifty years ago. Some rise to the challenge of finding beauty in the broad horizontal plain that resists reduction to the merely picturesque. Others in an autumn reverie can still imagine the Indians hiding behind the drying cornstalks. There are those who sense the generative power, immanent in so much growth. In the miles upon miles of corn rows that feed the nation, they see the promise of ethanol as well, to free us from petroleum dependence.

Photographers in Illinois, however, help people see the beauty in the landscape as it is now—fields that roll out as far as the eye can see, unbroken as the prairie by fenceposts or trees; farm buildings, grain elevators, and silos holding the amazing yield from the soil; small towns with main streets no longer "necessary" as farms become larger and larger and are supplied by truck. Some call attention to the fragile beauty of one way of rural life being transformed into another, capturing a landscape that is as much a relict as is a stretch of prairie along the railroad right-of-way in Champaign County. Also captured are the red barn and windmill against the blue sky, a souvenir of passing time—important to keep, because a historic landscape cannot be missed if it has never been appreciated. Some photographs of the West have lasted longer than the landscapes they framed.

The number of grain storage bins and elevators on the Illinois landscape suggests that the farmer has harvested more than he can market as raw product—if not more than the world can use. But

---

■ *One of the richest corn and soybean-producing counties in the Midwest, Champaign County is also home to the University of Illinois, an institution of international stature.*

Illinois ingenuity is at work again to transform this raw material into a finished product that can be exported. Corn is being turned into car fuel as ethanol; and in the near future, a non-corrosive de-icer for highways may be made of corn. Luckily, Illinois has never been bereft of ideas for better uses for a corn kernel, for a better mousetrap (Abingdon, Illinois, claims this one), or for a better plow—whose legacy became, and still is, big business in Illinois.

The challenge of taming the wild Illinois prairie was defined by the prairie sod that did not give up its secret easily, breaking many a plow. Plows that worked in lighter forest soils and rocky New England were ineffective in Illinois, where the loam clung to iron and wood. Originally from Rutland, Vermont, John Deere, a blacksmith in Grand Detour, Illinois, came to the rescue with a plow of polished steel in 1837, improving upon an idea of John Lane, Sr., of Lockport. Deere made and marketed thousands of plows to begin what would become a dominant industry in Illinois—and a much more dominant force on the land—agricultural machinery. Without Cyrus McCormick's reaper (1834)—a machine that replaced the scythe and cradle as a way to harvest grain—the increased production engendered by the rich prairie soil might have rotted in the field.

Necessity, the mother of invention, sometimes finds herself with a large brood. In Illinois, Joseph Glidden began the sale of a spurred, twisted fence wire that replaced the spiny Osage orange hedges originally introduced into Illinois as fencing in 1847 by Jonathan Turner of Jacksonville. Both kinds of fence were described as "horse high, hog tight, and bull strong."

The manifest destiny in the pioneers' restlessness for ever-new frontiers, which led to the Pacific Coast—and ultimately into Outer Space—was only part of the Illinois story. What happened in Illinois, the velocity with which it created itself, "like Minerva, sprung from the head of Zeus" (Ohio *Spy,* December 30, 1818), happened in part because Illinois was "west," but more because it became "middle." The men and women who stayed—as well as their inventions—transformed the Illinois landscape forever, but not without absorbing what has come to be called "the prairie spirit."

Early in its settlement, Illinois began to be a microcosm of the nation. According to Richard Jensen in *Illinois,* a visitor in 1830 described the state as "a complete mixture of almost every class of civilized men, from every part of the United States." Associating with a variety of persons promoted "liberality of sentiment," this visitor continued. "And this I consider a most happy circumstance."

The immigrants who became American in Illinois exchanged old landscapes, customs, and expectations for a vision that was unfettered. Mary Harvey wrote to her mother in England from Kaskaskia in 1844: "I am living in a finer country than ever my imagination had pictured to me as existing in this world." Consider "S" who wrote to his parents in England, "If you would give me my former situation, and pay my passage back, we are all in one mind, we would not return." Perhaps the Englishman Morris Birkbeck spoke for many, writing in his *Journey in America* and *Letters from Illinois:* "I *own* here a far better estate than I *rented* in England and am already more attached to the *soil.*"

Stephen A. Douglas, who came west to Illinois as a boy from New England, echoed them. In his opening remarks at the Jonesboro debate with Abraham Lincoln in 1858, he equated democratic vistas with the prairie, making it the quintessential American garden: "I . . . found my mind liberalized and my opinions enlarged when I got on these broad prairies, with only the heavens to bound my vision, instead of having them circumscribed by the little narrow ridges that surrounded the valley where I was born."

When the tall grass vanished in the wake of the plow, reaper, and man, it left more than "the loam of earth alive yet," as Carl Sandburg wrote in "The People Yes." A spirit remained underground like the prairie in winter, and was reborn in the culture's art, literature, and architecture, and in persistent attempts in the twentieth century to restore the prairie landscape.

■ *In the mid-nineteenth century, the romantic wildness of the prairie gave way to a neat patchwork of fields, best seen from above, as in a hot-air balloon over Verona in Grundy County.*

■ *Left:* At harvest time in DuPage County, pumpkins are often sold at roadside stands, to be turned into Halloween jack o'lanterns.
■ *Above:* Although predominantly rural, Tazewell County contains the major industrial center of Peoria, as well as Creve Coeur, *broken heart*, site of mid-America's first European settlement.

In the loam we sleep,
In the cool moist loam,
To the lull of years that pass
And the break of stars . . .

CARL SANDBURG

R.F.D. near Arthur, Moultrie County

■ *Above:* Only fifty years ago, corn left the field still on the cob; today, improved machines shell it before it leaves the field. ■ *Right:* McHenry County's many horse farms are an Illinois response to Kentucky bluegrass country. The county also contains a chain of glacier lakes and a scenic stretch of the Fox River.

Keep a red heart of memories
Under the great gray rain sheds of the sky,
Under the open sun and the yellow gloaming embers.
Remember all paydays of lilacs and songbirds;
All starlights of cool memories on storm paths.

CARL SANDBURG

Near Elburn, Kane County

■ *Left:* No longer a "sea of grass," some prairie survives in restoration projects and relicts such as this one in a cemetery near LaMoille in Bureau County. ■ *Above:* Untouched by the continental glaciers millions of years ago, this rolling vista near Woodbine is part of the "driftless area" in the state's northwestern corner.

On the left- and right-hand side of the road,
　　Marching corn—
I saw it knee high weeks ago—now it is head high—
　　tassels of red silk creep at the ends of the ears.

CARL SANDBURG

Farm entrance, Kane County

■ *Above:* Soybeans are a major crop in Ford County and rotate well with corn. ■ *Right:* Invented by Joseph Glidden of DeKalb, Illinois, twisted, or barbed, wire improved upon and then replaced the spiny osage orange hedge as fencing. Each kind of fence was described in its turn as "horse high, hog tight, and bull strong."

■ *Left:* A spider spins its web near Tuscola, which means "level plain," a comment on the flatness of its terrain. ■ *Above:* White oak, the official state tree, is found here in Coles County. The geographic and climatic range of Illinois favors more than thirty kinds of trees—from white pines at the northern border to bald cypress at the southern.

■ *Above:* Although beef cattle are raised all over the state, production is concentrated in western counties such as Jo Daviess. Poultry accounts for nearly one-third of the Illinois agricultural market. ■ *Right:* The hollyhock blooms from July to early September and is a common sight in cozy farmyards such as this one in Kendall County.

sometimes when the sky
overwhelms the world crimson
a man becomes the image of himself

JOHN KNOEPFLE

Near Arcola, Douglas County

■ *Left:* Originating in Asia and now grown on two-thirds of Illinois farms, the soybean is one of the oldest plants in cultivation. Along with corn, soybeans account for 87 percent of the crop sales in Illinois. ■ *Above:* Illinois is second in the nation in hog production, which comprises almost half of the state's livestock income.

Here the water went down,
   the icebergs slid with gravel,
   the gaps and the valleys hissed,
   and the black loam came,
   and the yellow sandy loam.

CARL SANDBURG

Along Illinois 47 near Fisher

■ *Left:* A variety of crops other than the predominant corn and soy-beans—which account for almost 90 percent of crop sales—are also grown in Illinois: wheat, barley, and oats, to name a few. ■ *Above:* Farming remains big business in Illinois, but requires different kinds of structures now that its scope is less local.

The prairie sings to me in the forenoon
and I know in the night I rest easy
in the prairie arms, on the prairie heart.

CARL SANDBURG

August cornfield near Yorkville

■ *Left:* A Fulton County farmstead near Lewistown contains a rare cross-gabled barn. The county is one of the state's most productive coal-mining areas. ■ *Above:* A morning walk begins the day near Arthur, an Amish trading center on the Moultrie and Douglas counties border, where the Illinois Amish community is concentrated.

■ *Above:* Farm life in Moultrie County revolves around the seasons—from seed-sowing through cultivation to harvest. ■ *Right:* Farmsteads, such as this one near Macomb in McDonough County, are often square to the road and surrounded by neatly plowed fields pieced together in the geometric patterns known as the grid.

■ *Left:* Among the most productive in the state, Mercer County land was so cheap and fertile that nineteenth-century settlers recouped their investment with one year's harvest. ■ *Above:* In pioneer days in Kendall County, the need for drainage tiles in readying the prairie for cultivation kept many a potter in business.

■ A stop sign at a country road near Lanark in Carroll County recalls the net of crossroads that covers most of the state. The Land Survey, ordered by Congress in 1795, made inevitable the triumph of geometry—a geometry defined by country roads and property lines, plowed fields and waving corn—over the tallgrass prairie.

CROSSROADS AND COMMON GROUND

Midway between the East and West, a splice of North and South—Illinois has always been a crossroads, as difficult to avoid by boat, wagon, or train in the nineteenth century as it is today by air or highway. The 1,110 miles of navigable waterways in Illinois established it early as a center for trade and, later, industry. Even the Indians, when they used these waterways, traded materials—large marine shells, obsidian, and even grizzly bear teeth—that suggest their paths reached the Gulf Coast and the Far West. In time, Illinois would become the hub of a complex transportation network—by rail, highway, and air—which would link it to every United States market and international port. This would prove a great advantage in the marketing and distribution of Illinois products.

However, people did not just pass through Illinois; they stayed. And they made the Prairie State the fastest growing state of the Union for much of the nineteenth century. The population of Illinois jumped from 55,221 in 1820 to 1,711,951 in 1860, an increase from twenty-fourth to fourth in population. By 1890, the state's population had almost tripled to 4,821,550. Native Americans "discovered" Europeans there. Immigrants became American there. Northerners and southerners, natives and immigrants, farmers and city slickers all met there and lent Illinois the remarkable diversity it is still known for. The soil was rich, and there was work. Railroads and canals needed to be built; plows and combines to be manufactured; people to be clothed, fed, and entertained; and paper to be shuffled. In short, a state was being created; and in the process, the landscape was being transformed by men and women whose handiwork, like that of the glaciers, would be most visible from the air.

Who knows why man goes up for a better view? In Illinois, he may have taken to the air because the sky was so much a part of the landscape. Still, he always comes down one way or another. In 1887, Thomas Scott Baldwin of Quincy, a nineteenth-century Evel Knievel, jumped from a hot-air balloon at four thousand feet with the aid of his invention—the flexible parachute—to the delight of the crowd below. By then, hot-air balloonists had been floating soundlessly above the Illinois landscape for thirty years; by then, the sea of grass had been surveyed.

All the great central prairie was open for cultivation by 1850, its rapid settlement made inevitable by the land survey of the Northwest Territory called for by a National Ordinance in 1785. Land was platted throughout Illinois and other states in rectangular parcels, based on townships six miles square, each with thirty-six sections consisting of 640 acres that could be further subdivided. A prospective landowner in Illinois, attracted perhaps by promoters' descriptions of its beauties, could purchase a land parcel located by a numbering system that was exact, if unromantic. John and Rebecca Burlend, who immigrated to Pike County from Yorkshire in 1831, secured for thirty-five pounds legal title to NE 1/4, NE 1/4 Section 6, TW 5 S, R 2W, 4 PM, or the northeast quarter of the northeast quarter of Section 6 in Township 5 south and Range 2 west of the fourth principal meridian. A clearer picture is drawn by Rebecca Burlend, who described it in, *A True Picture of Emigration* (1848): "an *improved* farm of eighty acres, with a log house and a stand of maple trees near the west bank of the Illinois River, south of Philips Ferry in Detroit Township."

Most visible from the air, the survey's grid was laid like a net across the land, neat rectangles created by roads and property lines, with farmsteads, churches, and towns accumulating at the corners throughout Illinois and the Midwest. A Cartesian geometry triumphed over the romantic wildness of the prairie, to be repeated in the cities and even in Chicago's skyscrapers. The corners became crossroads, and the crossroads, meeting points from which leaders who held common ground could arise.

In the 1850s, Illinois had little more than one hundred miles of railroad track; by the time Baldwin jumped, the landscape was sutured by more than seven thousand miles of track. By 1870, few communities and only 5 percent of the farms were more than ten miles from a train. Federal support for such transportation networks, as well as the Civil War, spurred the population boom in Illinois between 1850 and 1880. The building of both the Illinois and Michigan Canal and the railroads attracted industries—like the stockyards and coal mines—and immigrant workers as well: Irish, Italians, Poles, Germans, Lithuanians, Jews, Chinese, Norwegians, Swedes, Russians and Czechs. In the 1850s, more than one-third of its population was foreign-born, and the rest had been born elsewhere in the United States. Illinois was becoming a state that strained to contain its heterogeneity. Although Chicago is most noted for its ethnic diversity, immigrants left marks all over the state, and their heritage can be seen in such place names as German Valley, Hamburg, Swansea, New Athens, Vienna, and Zion, Verona, Rio, Havana, and Waterloo.

Illinoisans today are still surprised on occasion by adventurers who parachute into traffic on Michigan Avenue or who scale tall buildings like the famous daredevil, "Spiderman." Such stunts notwithstanding, public life in Illinois today bears little resemblance to life in Quincy in 1858. Then, the only show in town was the series of legendary debates scheduled between candidates for a Senate seat. In seven communities, one in each of the Illinois Congressional districts—Galesburg, Freeport, Ottawa, Charleston, Alton, Quincy, and Jonesboro—Abraham Lincoln and Stephen A. Douglas debated the issue of the extension of slavery. In today's era of carefully choreographed television debates, the Lincoln-Douglas debates are almost unimaginable.

For the first debate, on August 21, 1858, in Ottawa, people poured in by wagon, rail, and canal, swelling the town. Military companies were out. Bands played. Artillery thundered; and supporters of long Abe, a native of Kentucky, and the "Little Giant," paraded the street in anticipation of the debate which would last more than four hours in the courthouse square. In the series in general, Douglas argued for the right of people to decide whether their state would allow slavery. Lincoln reiterated his famous contention—originally delivered at the 1858 Republican Convention—that "a house divided against itself cannot stand. I believe this government cannot endure permanently half slave and half free." Although Douglas was reelected to the Senate, Lincoln gained national prominence as a worthy opponent of the skilled orator Douglas. Two years later, when these same sons of the prairie ran for president, the young lawyer defeated the silver-tongued orator. Thrust into a position of holding the "house" together, arguably the most difficult national conflict ever, President Lincoln had the support of his fellow Illinoisan until Douglas's untimely death in 1860.

It has been said that Illinois contains so many opposites that, by necessity, it has become a state of compromises and mergers. However, when the national conflict was mirrored in a state that gave soldiers to both the Union and the Confederate armies, the national leader that emerged from this cauldron of values was uncompromising about the sanctity of the Union.

It was not unusual that political debates took place at courthouses, for the courthouse was the acknowledged meeting place in a county, even for visiting preachers "who may there collect an audience and rave or reason as he sees meet," according to Morris Birkbeck, who immigrated to the Wabash Valley from England at the turn of the nineteenth century. Illinoisans can still meet this part of their past in a variety of historic courthouses at Thebes, Metamora, Mount Pulaski, and Lincoln, as well as in Cahokia, where the courthouse (circa 1790) is the oldest surviving building in the Midwest.

In Illinois, no one is ever very far from common ground with Abraham Lincoln and the grand themes of freedom, equality, and unity for which he stood. The many sites associated with Lincoln in the capital of Springfield alone include the Old State Capitol where he served as a state legislator and delivered his "House Divided" speech; the Lincoln-Herndon Law Offices; and the only home he ever owned—a site now maintained by the National Park District.

■ *Common in DeKalb County, the familiar winged ear of corn advertises more than a specific corn seed company. It also touts Illinois ingenuity in making a better corn kernel.*

Just outside of Springfield is the re-creation of New Salem Village where he spent his young adulthood. Near Charleston is the grave of his father, Thomas Lincoln—whose simple marker reads, "[his] humble but worthy home gave to the world Abraham Lincoln." Finally, near Bement, is Bryant Cottage—where Lincoln and Douglas hammered out the terms of their series of debates.

But Lincoln is not the state's only notable leader, nor are communities associated with Lincoln the only places to explore the rich heritage of the state. Many people left their mark on Illinois in a variety of ways. For example, Illinoisans can find the legacy of Ulysses S. Grant in Galena; Carl Sandburg in Galesburg; Edgar Lee Masters along the Spoon River in Lewistown; Vachel Lindsay in Springfield; and Jane Addams at Hull House on Chicago's West Side. Moreover, present-day encounters with the past in Illinois recall the turbulence of its history. The elegant monument in Alton to Elijah Lovejoy belies the violence that took his life for his anti-slavery editorials. The Haymarket and Pullman districts in Chicago call up a clash of languages and cultures that contributed to labor turmoil as Illinois rapidly became an industrial force in the nineteenth century.

Various historic sites provide today's Illinoisans with an opportunity to meet the successive generations who invented their state. Illinois is rich with archaeological evidence of prehistoric civilizations—in Fulton County at Dickson Mounds, or at Kampsville in Calhoun County—where the Mississippi and Illinois rivers join. However, nowhere is the encounter with prehistoric Illinois more dramatic than near Collinsville, at Monk's Mound. Once the focal point for a city of twenty-five thousand people (circa A.D. 1200), Monk's Mound is the largest flat-topped mound north of Mexico. Not far south of Monk's Mound, Illinoisans meet their French and British colonial past during an annual rendezvous at Fort de Chartres— once the westernmost outpost of the French empire in the New World. The formidable statue of Blackhawk by Lorado Taft in Lowden State Park, near the town of Oregon, allows one to meditate

on the earlier inhabitants—who fiercely fought to remain stewards of a land they could not view as property to be owned.

For some, Illinois meant religious freedom. For example, the town of Bishop Hill was founded in 1846 as a Swedish utopian community led by Erik Janson. It lasted as a religious commune for little more than a decade. Restored by descendants of the Jansonists, today it evokes life on the prairie for a host of visitors through an excellent museum and a world-famous collection of primitive paintings by Olaf Krans, which depict life in Bishop Hill in its heyday.

Nauvoo, once the largest city in Illinois, was the site for two groups seeking religious freedom on the prairie—the Mormons and the Icarians. In 1839, under the leadership of Joseph Smith, the Mormons settled in this town on the Mississippi River. By 1844, the Mormon Church was in conflict, and non-Mormons grew increasingly wary of the community's success and Smith's power. Soon after, he and his brother were killed by a mob in the Carthage jail, and Brigham Young led the colony west to Utah. Today, visitors can encounter the confluence of Illinois history with one of the nation's most significant indigenous faiths. Original buildings from the settlement, ruins of the temple, and the graves of Joseph and Hyrum Smith, have been restored by two branches of the Mormon Church.

After the Mormons left Nauvoo, the Icarians, a French utopian group led by Étienne Cabet, settled in the town. Like the Jansonists, they established a short-lived commune, which dissolved in 1857. The Illinois Amish—descendants of the original Amish who settled in the state in the 1830s and 1840s—continue to thrive as a community near Arthur in Moultrie County.

Illinoisans still share some of the nineteenth-century delight in festivals. In addition to such local celebrations as the Kewanee Hog Festival, the Urbana Sweet Corn Festival, the Grundy County Corn Festival, and the Clinton Apple and Pork Festival, each of the state's 102 counties has an annual fair. However, none matches the Illinois State Fair in Springfield, which is the largest agricultural exhibition

■ *Rising from the landscape like cathedrals, grain elevators are believed to be a midwestern, if not an Illinois, invention. Once made of wood, today they are often constructed of concrete or steel.*

in the world. All these events highlight the agricultural heritage of Illinois and draw people from all over the state, even political candidates in election years.

Where do Illinoisans meet their prairie heritage? In part, Illinoisans can meet the prairie in all who drew inspiration from the spirit of this quintessential American place, a spirit that was recognized even as the prairie disappeared. "The prairie here in Illinois, in the heart of Lincoln's country, had a spirit of its own unlike the forest," as Francis Grierson wrote, looking back to a landscape passed, in his *Valley of Shadows* (1909). The prairie spirit can be found in the words of writers such as Carl Sandburg; it also can be found in the buildings of Louis Sullivan and his protege, Frank Lloyd Wright—who led the Prairie School. This short-lived architectural movement borrowed from the great vista—the "quiet level," as Wright called it—of the midwestern landscape. However, after World War I, even this man-made movement named for the land vanished. Thus the break with the prairie heritage of Illinois was virtually complete.

Yet, the formula for creating a prairie perennially teeming with life is simple, according to Emily Dickinson:

> To make a prairie it takes a clover
> and one bee —
> One clover, and a bee,
> And revery.
> The revery alone will do
> If bees are few.

Poetic license aside, where then are the large prairie parks in Illinois? For the most part, they no longer exist. A barrier that proves more formidable than funding for restoration is the barrier of an inherited landscape, which precludes an appreciation of what came before. It is an old story. "How can people miss what they have never known?" asks Floyd Swink, plant taxonomist at the Morton Arboretum in Lisle. For Swink, "it is a failure of education," and a missed opportunity. "With a different land ethic, we could have had a prairie preserve, a two-mile-wide strip of prairie, perhaps, from Manitoba to Texas, a natural habitat for bison."

It is true that prairies, however small, engender fantasies of never-ending tides of grass borne out to the horizon by something like the pull of the moon. But dreams do not have to suffice. Luckily, prairies can be recovered as natural areas—with enough effort. Land can be taken out of cultivation, seeds from existing prairie plant communities collected and planted, interloping weeds removed year after year, and fields burned periodically to allow the sun to encourage the full range of prairie growth. In other words, the land can be transformed into a prairie with industry, knowledge, and imagination—in a matter of years rather than eons.

Compared to the thousands of acres of prairie that early pioneers encountered in Illinois, the two thousand or so acres that remain are little more than a bee and some clover. But they are very welcome. At the Morton Arboretum, the twenty-five-year-old prairie restoration project, containing more than two hundred plant species, is a heavily visited site. It is now a self-maintaining community of prairie plants—big bluestem, coreopsis, shooting star, among others.

Within the circumference of the atom smasher at the Fermi National Accelerator Laboratory outside of Chicago, Bob Betz—a professor of biology at Northeastern University—has led a corps of volunteers since 1975 in restoring to tallgrass prairie the six hundred acres above the accelerator's underground ring. Conservationists in suburban Markham hope to oversee, parcel by parcel, the creation of a five-hundred-acre Indian Boundary prairie preserve that would become one of the largest in the state. These restorations are a new form of land stewardship, a new kind of historic site.

Illinoisans may never be able to see a living prairie carpet spread before them for fifty miles in all directions—or even a historic photograph of the summer prairie. Bit by bit, however, they can begin to meet their prairie past—not just in a summer reverie.

■ *New Salem State Park is just outside of Springfield, the state capital. Within the park, New Salem village has been restored to the way it was when Abraham Lincoln lived there as a young man.*

The top of the ridge is a cornfield.
It rests all winter under snow.
It feeds the broken snowdrifts in spring
To a clear stream cutting down hill to the river.

CARL SANDBURG

Winter field west of Geneva

■ *Left:* Lewistown, the Fulton County seat, was the site of the boyhood home of Edgar Lee Masters. ■ *Above:* From A.D. 800 to 1500, Indians who lived near what is now Collinsville built hundreds of earthen mounds. The most imposing, Monk's Mound, has been named as a World Heritage site, one of only 120 so designated by UNESCO.

■ *Above:* The U.S. National Cemetery near Mound City is a resting place for the Illinoisans who fought in the Civil War: some wore blue and some wore grey. ■ *Right:* Abraham Lincoln's body came to rest at the Oak Ridge Cemetery after a cross-country funeral procession by train. The present 117-foot memorial was completed in 1874.

ISAAC BURNER RESIDENCE
Burner was born in Kentucky on September 24, 1784. Isaac, his wife Susan and his family moved to New Salem in October 1832, where he bought two lots for $10 and erected a residence. His daughter Elizabeth, married Isaac Gulihur, whose homesite is to the west of here. Isaac's son, Daniel Green Burner worked at the 2nd Berry-Lincoln Store for a short while. The Burner family left New Salem in 1835 when they moved to the country about six miles south of Knoxville, Illinois. A common feature of early log homes was the sleeping loft like the one here.

■ *Left:* When New Salem village was re-created in the 1930s, care was taken to use original building materials, such as black walnut, and red and white oak. ■ *Above:* It was from Nauvoo, situated on the Mississippi River, that Brigham Young led the Mormons west to Utah after Joseph Smith was killed in Carthage Jail in 1844.

and on the ground, a stillness,
the fields pieced neatly in squares,
the perfectly parallel rows of corn,
the right angle lines of fence . . .

BRUCE GUERNSEY

Plowed field off I-57, Cumberland County

■ *Above:* Time forgot the town of Galena when the lead ore mines that made it a boomtown played out. Today, visitors come to see the many mansions, with porticoes and cupolas to spare, that attest to its antebellum prosperity. ■ *Right:* A rose bush and white picket fence— both symbols of home—adorn many cozy yards in Lake County.

Wonder as of old things
Fresh and fair come back
Hangs over pasture and road.
Lush in the lowland grasses rise
And upland beckons to upland.

CARL SANDBURG

Orchard near Murphysboro, Jackson County

■ *Left:* Floating soundlessly over corn and soybean fields, hot-air balloons rally near Macomb in McDonough County, home of Western Illinois University. ■ *Above:* Only an hour from Chicago, Fox River Valley in Kane County, once cherished by the Fox Indians, is dotted with many tree-shaded towns of large homes and expansive lawns.

The people know what the land knows
the numbers odd and even of the land
the slow hot wind of summer and its withering
or again the crimp of the driving white blizzard

CARL SANDBURG

Amish buggies, Douglas County

■ *Above:* Abandoned pumps have given way to stations at a relatively new kind of crossroad—interstate and county road—in Clay County.
■ *Right:* Set on the eastern bluff of the Mississippi River, Quincy is still a thriving commercial center, much as it was when Governor John Wood's mansion was built there in the nineteenth century.

■ *Left:* A stone marker commemorates the donation of land for a school in rural Bellflower in McLean County. In the heart of the state's corn belt, McLean County is also home to both Illinois State and Illinois Wesleyan universities. ■ *Above:* The Mississippi River joins the Ohio River at Cairo, the state's southernmost point.

■ *Above:* Named for Thomas Jefferson's home in Virginia, Monticello draws people from all over Piatt County to its Friday night square dance, an American tradition. ■ *Right:* The Rialto Square Theatre in Joliet was built in the 1920s as an entertainment palace. With seating for two thousand, it is now used as a cultural center.

■ *Left:* The Old State Capitol in Springfield has been the site of many famous speeches, including Lincoln's famous "House Divided" speech in 1858. ■ *Above:* The rotunda of the current capitol, completed in 1887, is a kaleidoscope of history. Its statues of famous Illinoisans remind visitors of the state's great leaders.

■ *Above:* Historic Galena attracts antique buffs looking for a window on nineteenth-century America. ■ *Right:* Founded by Erik Janson in 1846, Bishop Hill has been restored by descendants of the Swedish Utopians. The Colony Church houses a collection of paintings by Olaf Krans depicting communal life during the town's heyday.

Never came winter stars more clear
yet the stars lost themselves
midnight came snow-wrought snow-blown.

CARL SANDBURG

Fresh snowfall, DuPage County forest preserve

■ *Above:* Founded in 1853, Wheaton College in DuPage County is one of the state's many fine liberal arts colleges. ■ *Right:* An unusual edge-supported dome four hundred feet in diameter, the Assembly Hall on the campus of the University of Illinois at Champaign-Urbana is usually filled for various sporting and cultural events.

CITY IN A GARDEN

In Chicago, in 1952, then Governor Adlai Stevenson welcomed the delegates of the Democratic National Convention with a speech that echoed those of previous Illinois men and women, whose roots, deep in Illinois, sustained them as they sought national and international leadership roles:

> Here, my friends, on the prairies of Illinois and the Middle West, we can see a long way in all directions. We look to east, to west, to north and south. Our commerce, our ideas, come and go in all directions. Here there are no barriers, no defenses to ideas and to aspirations. We want none; we want no shackles on the mind or the spirit, no rigid patterns of thought, and no iron conformity. We want only the faith and conviction that triumph in fair and free contest.

The convention that began with this invocation of the prairie spirit—where open vistas and the democratic impulse are powerfully wed—culminated with Governor Stevenson becoming the state's first presidential nominee since Ulysses S. Grant. Also a presidential candidate in 1956, Stevenson became one of the United States' most honored Ambassadors to the United Nations.

By any measure, the view from Chicago was impressive in 1952. Not even one hundred years after the Great Fire, it was home to more than three and one-half million people—a prairie metropolis, the heart of the nation's industrial market, as well as its breadbasket.

Despite an unpromising debut as a trading post situated where a sluggish river entered into a lake, Chicago was in a position to serve a developing nation. As one visitor put it in 1820, Chicago would be "a depot for the inland commerce, between the northern and southern sections of the union, and a great thoroughfare for strangers, merchants, and travelers." Location. Location. Location. In classic real estate argot, Chicago had it all. Given its location, almost everything passes through here: poets on their way to readings, horseradish for corned beef sandwiches in delis all over the country, even the Academy Awards, for the "Oscars" are made on Chicago's

north side. Nearly one-third of the nation's gross national product is created within a three-hundred-mile radius of Chicago.

Jean Baptiste Point du Sable, whose mother was Haitian and whose father was French, is considered to be the first Chicagoan. In 1800, he sold the trading post he established there to Jean la Lime, in what was the earliest real estate transaction recorded in Chicago. Today, a museum of Afro-American History bears du Sable's name and attests to the important role of blacks in the history of Chicago.

Chicago was made "safe" for settlement when, in 1833, a grand council of Potawatomi, Ottawa, and Chippewa chiefs ceded their lands and moved across the Mississippi to Indian reservations, together with the few remaining Illiniwek. Illiniwek meant *the men*—"as if other tribes were animals," as Marquette observed. No known descendant of an Illinois tribe can be identified, nor can the date of their extinction be traced.

Legend has it that bankers from both Galena—a booming lead mining town on the Fever River—and Shawneetown—still the Gateway to the West on the Ohio River—turned down an opportunity to invest in fledgling Chicago. They could hardly be blamed. Despite its promise, Chicago had a population of only fifty in 1830. By the time of its official charter in 1837, Chicago was beginning to look a bit more like a city than a swamp—with a population that had grown to 4,170. The ingenuity that tamed the prairie also built Chicago from a village to a city in what seemed like the blink of an eye. By 1850, Chicago's population was "ballooning," as a result of a new method of construction that replaced joists of mortises and tenons with thin plates and studs that were held together with nails. One of the first of Chicago's architectural innovations, this method was called "balloon frame" by its critics—who were alluding to its potential flimsiness—and "Chicago construction" by those who recognized its role in building the city. By 1850, with thirty thousand people, Chicago already had a meat-packing plant, factories, and warehouses.

■ *When it was built in 1925, Union Station was touted as the most modern railway station in the world. It is still a hub for both cross-country and commuter trains to and from the city.*

By 1870, nine railroads ran to the Union Stockyards southwest of the city, and a small canal connected it with the river. There, two million four hundred thousand hogs—each "15 or 20 bushels of corn on four legs"—and five hundred thousand cattle were received in 1871. In building the railroads, the I and M Canal, and stockyards, immigrants also built the city. Completed in 1848, the I and M Canal connected the Des Plaines and Illinois rivers, and ran through eighteen Chicago neighborhoods and thirty-eight Illinois communities, spanning 120 miles between Bridgeport and La Salle. Today, it is a National Heritage Corridor, an urban cultural park, under the aegis of the National Park Service.

The lightning speed with which Chicago had grown to a population of three hundred thousand by 1870 caused it to be regarded as a natural wonder quite the reverse of legendary Atlantis. "A city heaved up out of the mud by a benevolent earthquake," was how one British visitor put it.

By 1871, however, the city's remarkable development was hobbled. With the speed and destruction of the autumn fires that once terrified settlers on the prairie, a blaze broke out on October 8, 1871. As legend has it, the fire began when a cow kicked over a lantern in Mrs. O'Leary's barn on the near west side. The flame spread swiftly north and east, consuming the dry tinder of wooden frame dwellings. For three days, Chicago became "a vast ocean of flames, sweeping in mile-long billows and breakers over the doomed city," according to one observer. Forever the measure of other disasters, the Chicago Fire gutted twenty-one hundred acres and left seventeen thousand five hundred homes and businesses in ashes. The homeless numbered more than one hundred thousand; three hundred people died.

If ever a place should have been named Phoenix, it is Chicago. Almost immediately after the fire, a second city was rising from the ashes. The central business district and north sides were gutted, but the south and west sides were untouched and able to give relief to the homeless. The railroads, the stockyards, the lumber companies, three-quarters of the grain elevators, and more than six hundred factories were still intact. Businesses such as McCormick's vowed to build again. On the good side, there was plenty of work to do and the will to do it. Cities that had counted Chicago down for the count in 1871, were knocked for a loop themselves by the city's rebirth. A second Chicago, with a taller skyline, was rebuilt in a rush of innovation that matched—and then overtook—its previous boom.

By 1880, five hundred thousand people lived there. By 1890, with the development and annexation boom, there were one million, making it another kind of second city—second only to New York in population. New transit systems hastened the city's expansion. Marshall Field, George Pullman, and Philip Armour built mansions south of the city on Prairie Avenue near 18th Street, now a historic district. A fashionable neighborhood grew up along West Washington Boulevard all the way to Garfield Park. It was a stunning green space laid out by Frederick Law Olmsted in 1869—an emerald in the city's necklace of parks.

By 1890, more than three-quarters of the city's population was foreign-born or first-generation American. As residents of modest and significant means moved to the circumference of the city, waves of newcomers settled in the core, drawn to Chicago by the promise of work in the stockyards and factories. Poles, Mexicans, Italians, southern blacks, and East European Jews followed the Bohemians, French, Germans, Irish, and Scandinavians who had come earlier.

The near west side was port of entry for this polyglot. Into this slum moved Jane Addams in 1889. The settlement house she founded, called Hull House, served the city's poor. There were nineteen nationalities in her political ward alone. This Nobel Peace Prize winner (1931) provided services that ranged from day-care to gymnasiums, social clubs to education programs that reached college extension level. Hull House became a far-reaching model for neighborhood improvement; and Jane Addams and her settlement

■ *At the north end of the Magnificent Mile of shops and residences, the humble Water Tower, now a tourist information center, remains as one of the few buildings to survive the Fire of 1871.*

workers became national champions for children's rights, among other causes.

Although the numbers of foreign-born have decreased, Chicago still has the largest Polish population outside of Warsaw and one of the largest Greek populations outside of Athens and Salonika. Hispanics—Puerto Ricans, Cubans, and Mexicans—are the fastest growing ethnic group. More Hispanics live in the Chicago area than in the border states of Arizona and New Mexico. But the city is also home to other groups, such as Hmong, Vietnamese, Koreans, Chinese, and Japanese. Blacks are the dominant ethnic group in the city. The late mayor, Harold Washington, won a stunning victory in 1982 as the first black mayor of Chicago. He was reelected for a second term, shortly before his untimely death in 1988.

Statistics, however, do not do justice to the experience of these people who helped build Chicago. They have found voice in a literature as diverse as are they. Upton Sinclair's *The Jungle*, James T. Farrell's *Studs Lonigan*, Finley Peter Dunne's *Mr. Dooley* series, Nelson Algren's *The Neon Wilderness*, Gwendolyn Brook's *A Street in Bronzeville*, and Richard Wright's *Native Son* all helped make the Chicago school of writing famous the world over. The image of Hull House in the shadow of the burgeoning metropolis is repeated in the theme of infinite possibility darkened by disappointment, so movingly struck in literature about Chicago. The black poet Langston Hughes asked, "What happens to a dream deferred? Does it dry up like a raisin in the sun?. . ." And that inspired Chicago-born Lorraine Hansberry to write her famous play about a black family who migrated to Chicago from the South. *Raisin in the Sun* won the New York Drama Critics' Circle Award as the best work in 1959, the first drama by a black woman to reach Broadway.

"Draw a circle of two hundred miles radius around Chicago," wrote H. L. Mencken in 1920, "and you will enclose four-fifths of the real literature of America—particularly four-fifths of the literature of tomorrow." In Chicago, Mencken's "tomorrow" is multi-ethnic, vital, contemporary literature, which rests on the legacy of previous writers—Henry Fuller, Francis Grierson, and Robert Herrick.

Yet the civic spirit that reimagined Chicago after the fire as a city with a place in the sun, not only as a commercial center but as a cultural center, is still a standard against which Chicagoans measure themselves. Sixty years after its debut as a trading post and only twenty years after a major portion of it had been ashes, Chicago hosted 27,539,000 persons from all over the world for the World's Columbian Exposition in 1893, honoring the four hundredth anniversary of the discovery of America by Columbus. Daniel Burnham, a well-known Chicago architect, directed the architects, artists, sculptors, and landscape architects—notably Frederick Law Olmsted—in creating a fantasy city of white plaster buildings. Classical in theme, the long driveways, fountains, artificial pools, and lagoons were backdrop for exhibits from forty-six nations, on six hundred thirty-five marshy acres south of the Loop—the downtown area so called because of its loop of elevated train tracks. To counter the Eiffel Tower of the Paris Exhibition, this World's Fair featured a giant revolving wheel invented by George W. G. Ferris of Galesburg, Illinois, which lifted forty persons in each of thirty-six cars, two hundred fifty feet above the "white city."

The innovative architecture for which Chicago was already known was not to be found in the "white city." To see this original architecture, the visitor had to stay downtown in the "grey city." By 1893, the first skyscrapers were up. Among the landmarks of the Chicago School were the Monadnock (1891), by Burnham and Root. Louis Sullivan called this imposing creation "an amazing cliff of brickwork." Sullivan was himself a student of one of the fathers of the modern skyscraper—William LeBaron Jenney. Along with Dankmar Adler, Sullivan completed the stunning Auditorium Theatre (1888) and the Carson Pirie Scott building (1899), with its intricate ornamentation. Some grand Chicago landmarks are vital constructions that still contain brisk activity today.

■ *Bustling with activity for most of the year—with bicyclists, joggers, picnickers—Chicago's lakefront is solitary in winter, when frigid weather prevails and ice accumulates along the shore.*

The name of one of Louis Sullivan's apprentices, Frank Lloyd Wright, would become synonymous with the Prairie School of architecture. Wright's buildings expressed the prairie spirit in a horizontal plane, with ornament more geometric than that for which Sullivan was known. The many buildings Wright left on the Illinois landscape include Robie House in Hyde Park and the Dana-Thomas House in Springfield. These architects have been followed by others who continue to make Chicago an "alfresco museum" of the history of modern and landscape architecture.

The planning genius that resulted in the World's Columbian Exposition, with its legacy of Jackson Park, was also brought to bear on the city itself. At the request of the Merchants Club, Daniel Burnham and Edward H. Bennett were commissioned to devise a plan for the future development of Chicago. "Make no little plans," Burnham argued. "They have no magic to stir men's blood and probably themselves will not be realized. Make big plans; aim high in hope and work, remembering that a noble logical diagram once recorded will never die but long after we are gone will be a living thing, asserting itself with growing intensity." Hardheaded and practical, the Plan looked at Chicago as a center of industry and traffic and anticipated the city's growth, making the report a classic document in city planning. Not all aspects of the Plan were implemented, but the lakefront parks and beaches were created, and a green belt of forest preserves acquired. Coupled with the ring of parks already planned for Chicago since the 1860s, these made the city's motto, *urbs in horto*, "city in a garden," a reality.

Chicago's stunning natural setting is a well-kept secret. Visitors are often surprised by the open green spaces in the city. This system of parks is the legacy of the many Chicagoans with a vision for the use of public lands. Daniel Burnham, Frederick Law Olmsted, Jens Jensen, Montgomery Ward, and Potter Palmer, among others, saw the parks as cultural sites as well as recreational areas. The city is set like a jewel in sixty-two thousand acres of forested picnic and recreational parkland. Its forest preserves cover over thirty-five hundred acres. In all, the city of Chicago has 572 parks, covering seventy-three hundred acres.

Looking east toward this "city in a garden"—from the vantage point of the tallest building outside the Loop—Chicago seems to accumulate mass gradually, as it rises from the plain. On hazy days, the skyline floats above the lake. No optical illusion, Chicago did gather itself up from the prairie. But now a web of communities, exceeding Chicago in population, has spun out from the central city. Just beyond the forest preserves that encircle Chicago, miles of low-rise residential areas, office parks, and loops of freeway and toll road spill out toward the horizon almost as far as the eye can see. Together, the central city with its seventy-seven neighborhoods and the surrounding suburbs—175 communities of comparable diversity—have become a new place, what geographers have called "a galactic metropolis." Approximately three hundred fifty thousand people commute from the suburbs to Chicago; about two hundred thousand Chicagoans commute to the suburbs for work. The flow from suburb to suburb grows yearly. Flexible and hardheaded as Burnham's plan of Chicago was, it did not predict the grand scale of this lively region. The space between the downtown Sears Tower and the west suburban Oak Brook Terrace Tower has become a new crossroads, one that challenges Illinoisans again "to make no little plans" for a common future.

Within the compass of this view lie two prairie restoration projects—at Fermilab and the Morton Arboretum, and now—Terrain. Located at O'Hare International Center in Rosemont, "Terrain" is a multilevel granite plaza/park containing twenty-two boulders ranging in weight from six to ten tons; three pools; and sixteen thousand plants from twenty-five species. It was built to depict the glacial movements that created the Midwest landscape.

Glaciers and prairie, land and people, crossroads and common ground—all still tell the story of Illinois.

■ *Within walking distance of this untitled sculpture by Pablo Picasso in Chicago's Daley Plaza, are works of sculpture by Joan Miro, Marc Chagall, Alexander Calder, and Jean Dubuffet.*

Winds of the Windy City,
Winds of corn and sea blue,
Spring wind white and fighting winter gray,
Come home here—they nickname a city for you.

CARL SANDBURG

The Chicago skyline from Lincoln Park

■ *Above:* In the "lake effect," wintry air causes steam to rise from Lake Michigan which still holds summer's warmth. ■ *Right:* Near Batavia, Fermilab—the world's most powerful atomic accelerator—anchors the Illinois Research and Development Corridor. Above the underground facility lie over three hundred acres of restored prairie.

The shuttlings of dawn color go soft
weaving out of the night of black ice
with crimson ramblers
up the latticed ladders of daytime arriving.

CARL SANDBURG

Along Lakeshore Drive near Chicago Harbor

■ *Left:* The United Airlines Terminal at O'Hare International Airport adds modern architecture to modern travel at one of America's busiest airports. ■ *Above:* St. Stanislas Kostka Church is the oldest of Chicago's Polish churches (1881). More people of Polish descent call Chicago home than any other place outside of Warsaw.

By day the skyscraper looms in the smoke and sun
and has a soul.
Prairie and valley, streets of the city,
pour people into it
and they mingle among its twenty floors
and are poured out again
back to the streets, prairies and valleys.

CARL SANDBURG

Illinois Central commuters near Grant Park

■ *Above:* Orchestra Hall, seating 2,546, is home for the world-renowned Chicago Symphony Orchestra. Considered to be acoustically perfect, Orchestra Hall was designed by Daniel Burnham and completed in 1904. ■ *Right:* Navy Pier is the site for the International Art Exposition, drawing crowds each year from all over the world.

■ *Left:* Chicagoans find pleasure in their city in all its seasons. However, they learn early to bundle up for winter games. ■ *Above:* During December, Daley Center is especially festive with a fanciful Christmas tree and ice sculptures. In the summer, there are farmers' markets, cultural exhibits, and brown bag entertainments.

■ *Above:* Morning sun in winter is especially prized along the icy lakefront, where highrises along Chicago's Lake Shore Drive are warmed by its rays. ■ *Right:* Each workday, downtown's Union Station spills out more than three hundred thousand commuters from communities as far-flung as Aurora, Crystal Lake, and Homewood.

Passers-by,
Out of your many faces
Flash memories to me
Now at the day end
Away from the sidewalks
Where your shoe soles traveled . . .

CARL SANDBURG

The Art Institute at Michigan Avenue

■ *Left:* Just north of the John Hancock Building, the neighborhood is called the Gold Coast, for its per capita income. ■ *Above:* Swimming, biking, and jogging are not the only kinds of activities made possible by Chicago's riviera; the luxurious lakefront allows for even a quiet game of chess in a pavilion near North Avenue Beach.

So between the Great Lakes,
The Grand De Tour, and the Grand Prairie,
The living lighted skyscrapers stand . . .

CARL SANDBURG

Early morning traffic, Lake Shore Drive

■ *Left:* Chicago's answer to the Latona Basin at the palace in Versailles, Buckingham Fountain is the focal point in Grant Park from May through October. ■ *Above:* A northwest view from the observation deck of the John Hancock Building shows city streets platted in a repetition of the grid that overlays rural Illinois.

Auburn autumn leaves, will you come back?
Auburn autumn oaks, foxprints burning soft,
burning the oaken autumn coats, burning
the auburn autumn fire—

CARL SANDBURG

The Morton Arboretum near Lisle

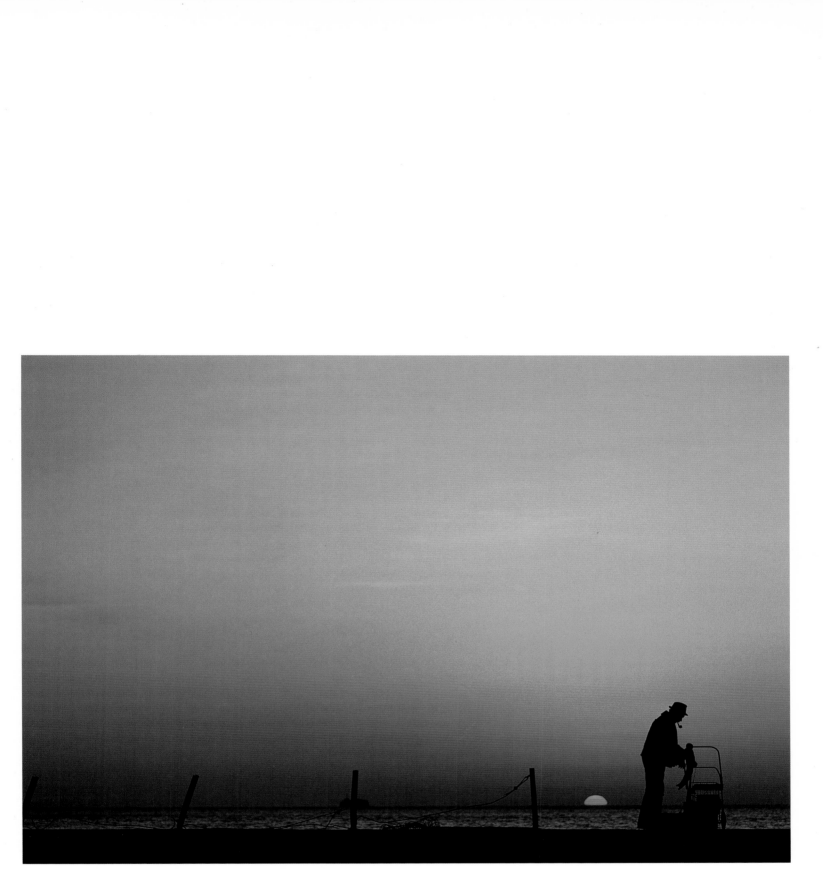

■ *Left:* Boats moored in Montrose Harbor on the city's north side may have different names, but all mean "feeling free." ■ *Above:* Of the city's many nicknames, the one that surprises visitors most is "city in a garden"—until they see the great parks and open spaces that ring the lakefront, creating quiet harbors of all kinds.

ACKNOWLEDGMENTS

Producing the images for this book on my home state has been a particularly rewarding experience. It has been a time of rediscovering a landscape of unique interest and beauty. Hopefully, it serves as a starting point for the reader's own investigation of this special place.

There are many who graciously assisted in my efforts to photograph the state. In particular, I would like to thank my brother, Mark, and his wife, Louanne, for providing me with a "home away from home" throughout the project. Special thanks also go to Bruce and Mary Beth Condill of Arthur, Wilbur and Thelma Giffhorn of Tremont, Herb Schmidt of Illinois Aerosports, Ed Taylor of Enchantment Balloons in Wilmington, Peggy Stapleton of the Rialto Square Theatre, Kevin Martin of the Chicago Symphony Orchestra, Dr. Robert Betz of Northeastern Illinois University, and Floyd Swink of the Morton Arboretum. Countless other individuals along the way have contributed their cooperation, assistance, and kind hospitality.

In addition, I would like to thank my friends at the Morton Arboretum for their moral support and encouragement.

My gratitude is extended especially to Kristina Valaitis for her energy and enthusiasm in an enjoyable collaborative effort, and to the staff of Graphic Arts Center Publishing Company, for their commitment to quality.

Most of all, though, I would like to thank my wife, Janine, and my children, Valerie and Emily, for their patience and love, and the Lord for His grace.

Gary Irving

I am indebted to the writers and photographers who have enlarged my appreciation of the Illinois landscape and especially to those who have worked to make more widely available such primary sources as settlers' accounts and early novels, now often out of print. Without them, the state's past could not be re-imagined. I owe special thanks, however, to one friend who introduced me to first-hand accounts of prairie Illinois and who always helps me see how much there is left to discover.

Kristina Valaitis